Lulu Mayo

HOW TO DRAW A
REINDEER
AND OTHER CHRISTMAS CREATURES

WITH SIMPLE SHAPES
IN 5 STEPS

Andrews McMeel
PUBLISHING®

FROM LULU

I hope you love the festive season as much as I do. Inside this book, I'll show you how to draw all the things that make Christmas the most wonderful time of year. This includes reindeer, jolly snowmen, festive llamas, and, of course, Santa.

Each magical creation is brought to life in five simple steps, using shapes that are easy to master. Don't worry if you make a mistake or your pictures look different from mine—all drawings are unique, and that's part of what makes them special. Have fun!

LULU MAYO

THE STEPS

The clear, step-by-step instructions for each creation in this book are easy to follow.

Outlining the body and head gives you a great starting point. Use a pencil to create your initial drawing.

Add simple shapes to start bringing your character to life.

1.

2.

3.

4.

Add all of the elements. Then erase the pencil lines you don't need.

Go over the outline in pen if you'd like.

5.

Finally, add color.

NOW PICK UP YOUR PENCIL AND DRAW!

1

SANTA CLAUS

1. start with a triangle
and a fluffy beard

2. add a face, semicircle nose,
and dots for eyes and mouth

3. rectangle body, with
triangles for arms and legs

4. draw in buttons
and a belt

5. color him in

Draw your Santa here. ⤵

2

Santa Claus is coming to town. Fill the page with Santas,
including some poking out of the chimneys.

Well, this is
embarrassing.

REINDEER

1. pear-shaped head and tooth-shaped body

2. dots for eyes, oval for nose, and circles for ears and snout

3. add antlers

4. add hair and a bow tie

5. fill with color

Now, you try.

Fill the sky with more reindeer.

CHRISTMAS TREE

1. three triangles with wavy bottoms

2. add dots for the eyes and a curved line for the smile

3. rectangle for the trunk and a star on top

4. decorate the tree

5. color it up

Have a go.

Turn this page into a Christmas forest.
Don't forget to dress up all the trees.

HEDGEHOG

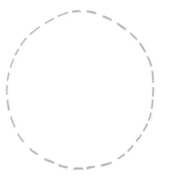

1. start with an oval
outline for the body

2. heart for face, circles for
ears and eyes, oval nose, and
lines for claws

3. add a scarf

4. make it really spiky

5. color it in

Your turn.

Doodle lots of hedgehogs in different poses.
Use the shapes below to help you get started.

It's party time!

SNOWMAN

1. three ovals

2. a cute facial expression

3. sticks for hands and ovals for shoes

4. hat, scarf, and buttons

5. add some color

Draw your own.

Get creative! Draw different faces on these snowpeople.

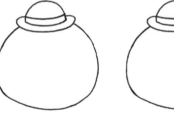

CAT

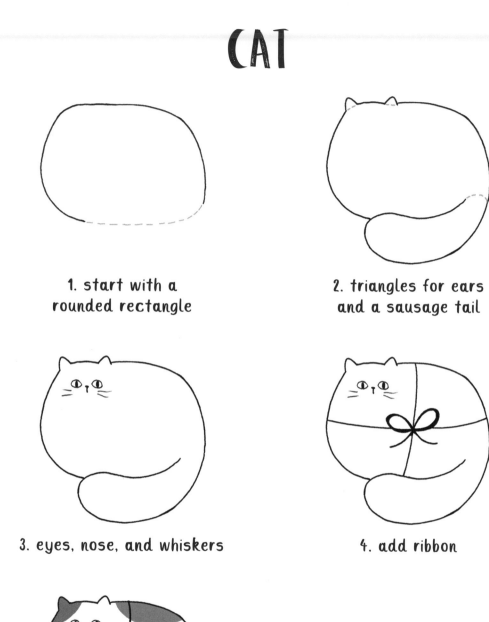

1. start with a
rounded rectangle

2. triangles for ears
and a sausage tail

3. eyes, nose, and whiskers

4. add ribbon

5. finish with a fun pattern

Give it a go!

Play with simple shapes to create more Christmas
cats. Why not wrap them up as well?

Zzzz . . . cat nap.

BADGER BAUBLE

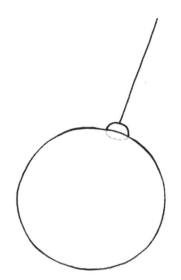

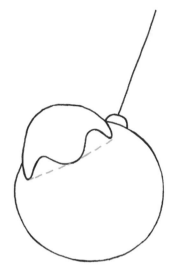

1. start with a line,
oval, and circle

2. add a semicircle
with a wavy line for
head and hands

3. circles for ears, dots
for eyes and mouth, and
oval for nose

4. rounded triangles
for legs and oval for tail

5. add black markings
and decorate

Now it's your turn.

Draw a collection of
Christmas decorations.

I'm having
a ball.

Doodle more fun patterns.

PANDA PRESENT

1. start with a
square and semicircle

2. add ovals for eyes and
nose and semicircles for ears

3. chubby triangular hands
and a reindeer antler
headband

4. tilted rectangle for lid

5. finish with a jazzy pattern

Give it a try!

Draw more presents, then wrap them
all up. What pattern will you pick?

Surprise!

SLOTH

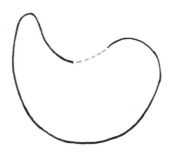

1. banana-shaped body

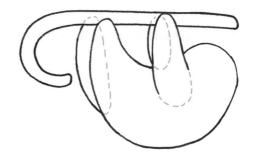

2. long ovals for arms and legs and a candy cane

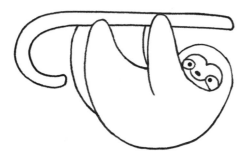

3. heart-shaped face and smiley expression

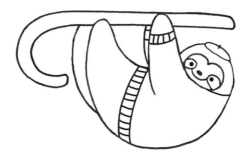

4. draw a beret and Christmas sweater

5. add some festive color

Create a sloth here.

Draw more festive sloths. Try using the left oval for
a hanging sloth and the right oval for a do-nothing sloth.

Cuddly
sloth

Do-nothing sloth

Hanging sloth

GINGERBREAD

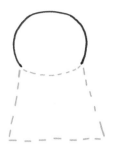

1. circle for the head and a trapezoid for the body

2. add oval hands and legs

3. circles for eyes, sausage for mouth, and eyebrows

4. add a bow tie and hat and dress it up

5. add a pop of color

Give it a try.

Experiment with these shapes to create lots of different ginger characters.

Stripy

Smiley

Happy

Bitten

UNICORN

1. start with three ovals

2. chubby triangles for legs and clouds for mane and tail

3. dots for eyes and nose and a stripy horn

4. add presents

5. finish with magical color

Draw your own.

Doodle more unicorns and horses. Add twinkly lights
and presents to make them extra Christmassy.

I've always
wanted a horn!

HAMSTER

1. a rounded,
upside-down heart

2. add dots for eyes and
a heart-shaped nose and mouth

3. circles for ears, triangles
for legs, and lines for claws

4. add a santa hat

5. add markings
and color it up

Sketch your own.

Use these shapes to draw more cute Christmas hamsters.

I hope you like it.

ELF

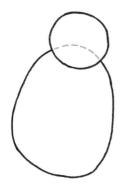

1. circle for head
and oval for body

2. add eyes, nose,
mouth, and wavy
line for hair

3. triangles for arms,
legs, and shoes;
rectangle for collar;
and dots for buttons

4. circle and triangle
for pointy hat

5. design your own
outfit and color it up

Your turn.

Play with circles, triangles, and ovals
to create different elf poses.

Santa!

PENGUIN

1. start with a
pear-shaped body

2. dots for eyes and triangles
for hands and nose

3. beanie, cross for a
belly button, and claws

4. rectangles for skis
and lines for poles

5. finish with color

Doodle your own.

Use these shapes to draw more penguins skiing or caroling.

Egg-shaped penguin

Draw your own caroling penguin.

Pear-shaped penguin

Bean-shaped penguin

RUSSIAN DOLL

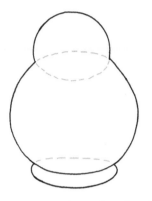

1. two circles for body and sausage for base

2. circle for face and wavy line for hair

3. eyes and mouth

4. add wavy lines

5. finish it with a festive design

Draw your own doll.

Can you fill the shelves with more Russian dolls or . . . animal dolls?

CHIPMUNK

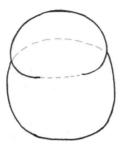

1. two ovals for
head and body

2. add triangles for ears
and a cute expression

3. circle for nut
and lines for claws

4. add a tail

5. scribble markings and
make it really fluffy

Give it a go.

Fill the woodland trees with more Christmas chipmunks.

I'm stuffed.

MOUSE MAIL

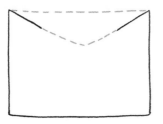

1. rectangle and upside-down triangle for envelope

2. semicircle for body, furry semicircle chin, and gloves

3. ovals for ears, eyes, mouth and a heart for nose

4. add whiskers and a triangle for back of envelope

5. color it up

Now it's your turn.

Try creating your mouse with different shapes. Don't forget
to fill the envelope at the bottom with a cute mouse.

Happy Christmouse!

ANGEL

1. oval for head, wavy line for bangs, and bell-shaped body

2. eyes, hair, and semicircle for nose

3. triangles for hands and legs and a trumpet

4. add wings

5. color in

Now you try.

Surround the tree with cute angels. Start with an oval or a circle and then add a bell or a trapezoid to vary their poses.

That trumpet sounds terrible.

LLAMA

1. curly hairdo and fluffy L-shaped body

2. banana-shaped ears, dots for eyes and mouth, heart for nose, and circle for muzzle

3. fluffy triangles for legs and a fluffy banana-shaped tail

4. draw Christmas lights and a bow tie

5. add a pop of color

Doodle your own.

Fill the page with adorable llamas. Why not style them with fun hairdos and Christmas costumes?

JINGLE RACCOON

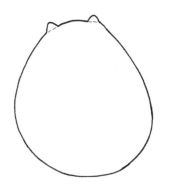

1. egg-shaped body and triangles for ears

2. heart-shaped face and cute expression

3. add bell

4. fat triangles for paws and an oval tail

5. color it in

Have a go.

Doodle more raccoons swinging on bells.

Ding-dong!

NUTCRACKER

1. rectangle for head and add eyes, nose, mustache, and mouth

2. fluffy beard and hair, circle, rounded square, and rectangle for hat

3. square and trapezoid for body, rectangle forearms, and semicircle hands

4. rectangles for legs and shoes

5. color it in

Time to try!

42

Can you fill the shelves with cute nutcrackers?
Try combining different shapes to create your own.

King nutcracker

Drummer nutcracker

OWL

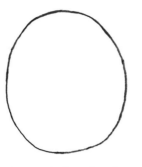

1. oval for body

2. hearts for face and wing

3. big eyes, heart for nose, and ears

4. add claws and mistletoe

5. complete it with color

Your turn.

Use the shape to create your own owl,
then draw more owls sitting on mistletoe.

T'wooo are you looking at?

POLAR BEAR

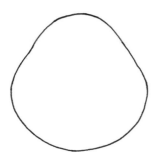

1. chunky pear shape for body

2. circles for ears, eyes, and mouth and oval for nose and muzzle

3. add hat and gloves

4. ovals for legs and Christmas sweater collar

5. color it up

Sketch your own.

Add more polar bears to the snow globe.

FAIRY

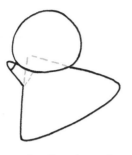

1. circle for head and triangles for hand and body

2. cute face, wavy bangs, and semicircle for bun

3. ovals for wings and triangles for legs

4. add a twinkly candy cane

5. dress her up

Draw your own fairy.

Doodle more adorable flying fairies all over the page.

ROBIN

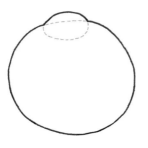

1. oval for head
and circle for body

2. S-shaped wing, dots
for eyes, and triangle beak

3. connect the wing and
add heart-shaped tail

4. add a hat and ice skates

5. color it up

Give it a go.

Use these shapes to draw more robins. Try varying
the starting shapes to create different poses.

Happy holly-days!

SNOWFLAKE

1. draw a star

2. add dots for eyes and a smile

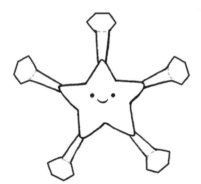

3. draw rectangles with hexagon ends

4. add rectangles with oval ends

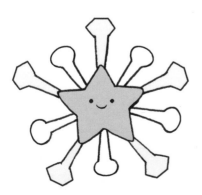

5. finish with colors

Your turn.

Fill the sky with lots of snowflakes.

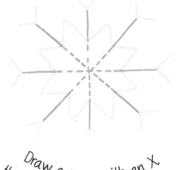

Draw a cross with an X through it to start your drawing.

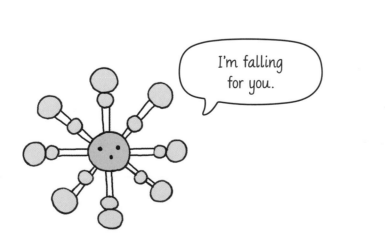

I'm falling for you.

WIENER DOG

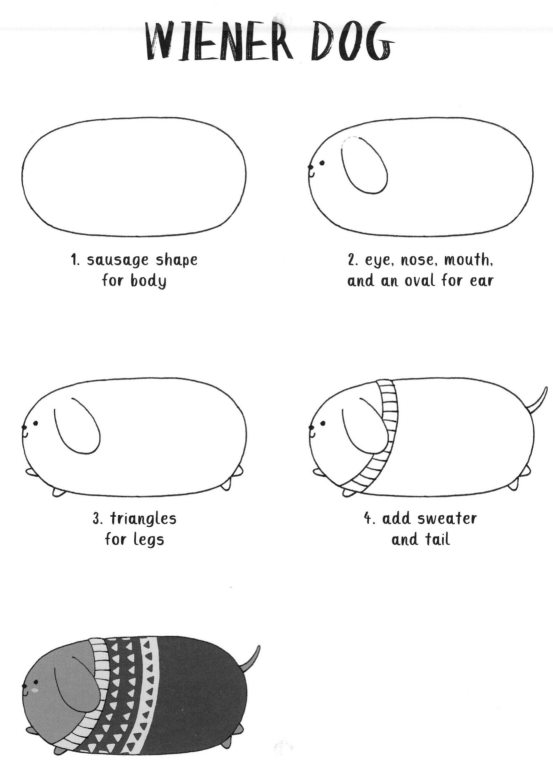

1. sausage shape
for body

2. eye, nose, mouth,
and an oval for ear

3. triangles
for legs

4. add sweater
and tail

5. color it up

Give it a try.

Experiment with these shapes to create more wiener dogs.

GINGERBREAD HOUSE

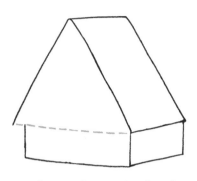

1. triangle and tilted rectangles

2. add frosting and a face

3. semicircle windows and oval door

4. semicircle roof tiles

5. decorate it the way you like

Give it a go.

Build more gingerbread houses in the snowy village.

Welcome!

RABBIT STAR

1. egg shape for body
and ovals for ears

2. eyes, nose, and a beanie

3. triangles for hands and
legs and a star

4. add a furry tail

5. color it up

Create your own.

Fill the space with more stars and rabbits. Can you
experiment with different shiny star patterns?

Time to shine!

WREATH

1. doughnut outline,
ribbon, and decorations

2. add pine needles

3. oval for fox's body
and a very bushy tail

4. triangles for ears
and a zigzag mane

5. dots for eyes and
nose then color it up

Doodle your own.

Design your Christmas wreaths. Don't forget
to decorate them with ribbons and lights.